# Ice cream

Mike Wheeler and David Byrne

This book is about how ice cream is made and stored, both now and in the past. It introduces some of the scientific facts behind making, keeping and cooking with ice cream.

If you are using the book to find out particular facts about ice cream, you do not have to read it all. Look in the **contents** (below) or the **index** (at the back) to find the best pages to help you. Then just read as much as you need to read.

The basic facts are given in big print, and more detailed information is in smaller print.

## Contents
| | |
|---|---:|
| 1  What is ice cream? | 2 |
| 2  How is ice cream made? | 6 |
| 3  How old is ice cream? | 10 |
| 4  Moving and storing ice cream | 14 |
| 5  Wrapping ice cream with food | 18 |
| Glossary | 22 |
| Further information | 23 |
| Index | 24 |

# 1 What is ice cream?

Ice cream is made from many things. Milk and sugar and other ingredients give it a taste and make it creamy. A lot of air is mixed into ice cream to make it light and fluffy. Without the air, ice cream would be very hard like an iced lolly.

⬆ The type of seaweed used in making ice cream.

Ice cream contains milk, sugar, fat and other ingredients. It also has a strange ingredient which comes from seaweed. Without seaweed, ice cream becomes very slushy. It is the seaweed ingredient that makes ice cream creamy.

It is strange, but in Britain ice cream does not need to have cream in it. Vegetable fat is often used instead. Ice cream which has cream in it is called dairy ice cream.

A lot of sugar is used in ice cream. There are two important reasons for this.

**1** Very cold things are difficult to taste. A lot of sugar means that it can be tasted more easily.

**2** The extra sugar also lowers the temperature of the ice cream. This means it stays frozen longer.

## All air and chemicals

When you buy ice cream, you are buying very little, or perhaps no cream at all. You are buying air, because nearly half the carton or box of ice cream is air which has been whipped in. Flavourings, colourings and special chemicals called stabilisers and emulsifiers are also added.

Chemicals keep the ice cream fluffy and soft.

When ice cream melts it loses its fluffiness.

Emulsifiers are special chemicals that allow different ingredients to mix easily together. Without them the cream and fats would not mix with the syrups and milk.

Stabilisers keep the ingredients mixed. Without them the different ingredients would begin to separate. One of the stabilisers is made from a seaweed called Giant Kelp. This ingredient stops the ice cream from going slushy.

Colours are also added to some ice creams. One of the most peculiar is a red or pink colouring called cochineal. This dye is made from the crushed bodies of a small red insect called the cochineal beetle.

Some of the ingredients, such as certain flavourings and colours, are not essential to ice cream. Some manufacturers are starting to leave these out because they are not very good for us.

You can now buy many different flavours of ice cream. The most popular flavours are vanilla, chocolate and strawberry. Many new flavours that are tried in the factories never reach the shops. One company even tried to make a curry-flavoured ice cream.

⬆ Ice cream is made in many colours and flavours.

# 2 How is ice cream made?

Ice cream can be made at home. It is not easy and it can take a long time. Most ice cream is made in a factory. Machines mix the ingredients together and then freeze them. The ice cream must be kept very cold to stop it from melting.

⬆ Special machines make whipped ice cream.

⬆ A machine mixes the ingredients of the ice cream.

In an ice cream factory, there are many machines. They all help to change the ingredients into frozen ice cream.

Many of the machines are controlled by computers. These computers make sure that the ingredients are mixed for the right length of time. They also make sure that the ice cream is frozen at the right temperature. They make sure that the right amount of ice cream is put into the carton.

The people who work in the factory check regularly that the computers are working properly.

⬆ Raisins are added by a machine to give flavour to the ice cream.

⬆ The machine lets just the right amount of ice cream pour into the carton.

7

# How factory ice cream is made

Making ice cream is a long and quite difficult process in a factory.

First of all, the dry ingredients are mixed together. These are modified starch, sugar, dextrose and vegetable fat. Then the liquids – skimmed milk, butter, oil and cream – are mixed in.

⬆ The ingredients of factory ice cream.

The mixture now has to be pasteurised. This means that it is heated up and then cooled down to kill all of the dangerous micro-organisms in it.

The mixture is homogenised, which makes sure that the ingredients are mixed or blended smoothly together.

Emulsifiers and stabilisers are added to stop the ingredients from separating.

The ice cream is then cooled to 2°C and put into a storage tank for a few hours where it is allowed to age.

⬆ In an ice cream factory there is a special room where pasteurisation takes place. It is kept very clean.

⬆ The ice cream is packaged and sealed before it is frozen.

Flavourings and colouring are added, and the mixture is sent to be frozen.

The last ingredients are then added. These are the chewy bits such as fruit, nuts or chocolate chips. At this stage, the ice cream is like the soft ice cream that you can buy.

Most ice cream is hardened. It is packaged in cartons and then stored in hardening rooms for four hours, where it is kept at about minus 27°C. The ice cream is then ready to be sent to the shop and sold.

# 3 How old is ice cream?

If you think that ice cream is something new, you are wrong. The Romans ate ice cream. Long before Roman times, the Chinese ate the first fruit ices. They were like iced lollies without a stick.

A Roman soldier eating ice cream.

In the Middle Ages, a famous explorer called Marco Polo visited China. His stories about life in China tell us that, the Chinese were eating ice cream then and had probably been eating it for many centuries. Marco Polo told people all about his travels and the frozen fruit ices he had seen.

They were probably made with crushed ice or snow, and fruit juice. It is likely that they were sweetened with honey. In Europe and Asia, the Early Persians and Arabs were known to have eaten sorbets.

⬆ A sorbet is similar to ice cream but it is made with water.

The Italians introduced ice cream to the rest of Europe. In 1533 an Italian served ice cream to the King of France. Italian ice cream is now famous across the whole world.

11

## The early ice creams

Ice cream could not be stored until freezing machines had been invented. Before freezing machines were used, the ice cream was placed in a box cooled with an ice and salt mixture. Ice and salt together produce lower temperatures than ice alone.

It was a long and difficult process. The temperature inside the box could not be kept very low, and the freezing took a long time. The first ice cream to be sold in shops was made by Jacob Fussel in 1851 in America, but it was not readily available until after 1900.

Ice cream cones were a special invention. They were made long after the first ice cream. In 1904 there was a world fair at St Louis in the United States of America. At the fair, a thin soft biscuit, called a waffle, was baked in the shape of a cone, until it was crisp. A scoop of ice cream was put into the waffle. This was the first ice cream cone ever served.

 Ice cream is sometimes eaten with a wafer biscuit.

It is surprising that the first ice creams were always hard, because it is easier to make soft ice cream. It was not until 1939 that the first soft ice cream was sold.

# 4 Moving and storing ice cream

Ice cream is taken from the factory to the shop in special lorries. These lorries have big refrigerators on the back. At the shop the ice cream is kept in a large freezer, because ice cream is spoiled if it melts. When people buy ice cream, they must take it home quickly before it melts.

⬆ Ice cream is delivered in refrigerated lorries.

⬆ The inside of refrigerated lorries are kept at a special temperature to keep the ice cream frozen.

Once ice cream has melted, it must not be frozen again. In fact, it is illegal to sell ice cream that has begun to melt, because micro-organisms will start to grow on it. Ice cream must get to the shops while it is still frozen.

To do this refrigerated lorries and vans are used. These are lorries with fridges on the back of them. The fridges are so big that a person can walk inside them. They are well insulated to keep the heat out. They also have a special power unit on them which keeps the temperature of the fridge very low.

Ice cream in shops must be kept in freezers. They usually have clear plastic lids. This allows shoppers to choose what they want without having to open the top of the freezer and letting warm air in.

## Wrapping and storing ice cream

Most ice cream used to be wrapped in waxed card and sold in blocks from the local shop. Individual ice cream was wrapped in waxed paper.

It is now all different. Ice cream is sold mainly from supermarkets, and it is nearly always in a plastic tub with a sealed lid. Unlike the old waxed cardboard, the sealed packaging or tub stops any melted ice cream from running out.

Plastic has replaced wax card and even ice lollies are sealed in plastic wrappers. The plastic has to be chosen very carefully so that it does not harm the taste of the ice cream.

In the past, ice cream was sold from tricycles with a cold box on the front of them. The cold boxes were well insulated and often filled with ice or frozen carbon dioxide, known as dry ice. These two things kept the contents cool.

Tricycles are beginning to make a comeback in some seaside towns.

# 5 Wrapping ice cream with food

Ice cream melts quite quickly, but if it is wrapped it will stay frozen for longer. The wrapping keeps the heat out. An Arctic Roll is an ice cream which has cake wrapped around it. The cake stops the ice cream from melting too quickly.

The ice cream in an Arctic Roll does not melt easily.

⬆ The bubbles in the sponge cake insulate the ice cream.

An Arctic Roll is hard ice cream which has been wrapped in a sponge cake. As sponge cake mixture is cooked, it forms lots of tiny bubbles inside it. These air-filled bubbles do not let heat through easily. This means that the sponge cake is a good insulator. It keeps the cold in and the heat out.

Ice cream served in this way can stay on the table for much longer than ordinary ice cream, before it begins to melt.

# Ice cream in the oven

Ice cream can be placed in a hot oven without melting. This can work with the help of insulators. *Baked Alaska* is made using what we know about insulators.

**1** Ice cream is placed on a round sponge cake as a base.

**2** Egg whites are whipped so that air is trapped in bubbles inside it.

**3** All of the ice cream and sponge is coated with the egg whites so that it is covered with trapped air bubbles.

**4** The *Baked Alaska* is then cooked. The egg whites turn brown but the ice cream is still frozen because it has been protected or insulated by the air bubbles surrounding it.

⬆ The ice cream is insulated at the bottom by the sponge.

⬆ Egg whites are beaten to make them full of air.

**3**

⬆ The ice cream is insulated at the top by the beaten egg whites.

**4**

⬆ The ice cream is still frozen inside the *Baked Alaska*.

**21**

# Glossary

**Arabs**
Arabs are people who live in the part of the world called Arabia.

**Carbon dioxide**
Carbon dioxide is a gas. It is found in the air.

**Early Persians**
The Early Persians were people who lived in the part of the world that we now call Iraq.

**Emulsifiers**
Emulsifiers keep food together so that it does not separate.

**Flavourings**
Flavourings are ingredients that help to change the taste of food.

**Homogenised**
Milk that is homogenised will not form a layer of cream at the top of a bottle. This is because the cream has been fully mixed into the milk.

**Insulators**
An insulator is something that doesn't allow heat to pass through it. It can keep hot things hot and cold things cold.

**Ingredients**
Ingredients are all the things that are needed to make something.

**Melting**
If ice cream is left in a warm place it will soon become runny. When it becomes runny we say that it is melting.

**Micro-organism**
A micro-organism is a tiny living thing which cannot be something seen with your eye. It can only be seen by using a microscope.

**Pasteurised**
Pasteurised milk has been heated to a high temperature and left to cool. This process makes milk safe to drink.

**Refrigerator**
A refrigerator is a machine which keeps things very cold. It is often called a fridge.

**Salt**
Salt is a chemical. It is found in sea water. It is added to food to bring out the flavour.

**Sorbet**
A sorbet is a frozen food. Fruit, sugar and water are used to make it.

**Vegetable fat**
Fat is found in many foods. Some plants have fats in them. Nuts, and sunflower seeds are examples. Fats from a plant are called vegetable fats.

**Waxed paper**
Waxed paper is paper that is covered with a shiny wax. It is a very useful food covering because foods will not stick to it.

# Further information

## Books

*Hot and cold* by Peter Mellett and Jane Rossiter, Franklin Watts.

*Liquids in Action* by Peter Mellett and Jane Rossiter, Franklin Watts.

*Children's Illustrated Encyclopaedia*, Dorling Kindersley.

*Fun with Science – Simple Chemistry* by Steve Parker, Kingfisher.

*Chemistry in the Kitchen* by Beverley Le Blanc, Cherry Tree Books.

## Places to visit

The Science Museum, London.

# Index

**Aa** air 2, 4
Arctic Roll 18, 19

**Bb** Baked Alaska 20, 21

**Cc** China 11
colours 5
cones 12

**Ee** emulsifiers 4, 8

**Ff** factory ice cream 6, 7, 8, 9
flavourings 4, 5, 9
freezer lorries 14, 15
freezers 14, 15

**Ii** Italian ice cream 11

**Mm** Marco Polo 11
micro-organisms 8, 15

**Ss** seaweed 3, 4
sorbets 11
stabilisers 4, 8

**Tt** tricycles 17

**Ww** waffles 12
wrappers 16

a b c d e f g h i j k l m n o p q r s t u v w x y z
A B C D E F G H I J K L M N O P Q R S T U V W X Y Z